WHO WAS JESUS?
Myrtle Langley

It's a very special day — Christmas Day. All over the world Christians are celebrating the birth of Jesus Christ — which took place almost 2,000 years ago. They are celebrating a birth which changed history. For many people around the world, whether or not they are Christians, it is a public holiday, a time for giving and receiving presents, for enjoyment and rejoicing.

But that birth was not the end of the story — it was only the beginning.
Most people know something of the Christmas story — of a baby born in a stable, of angel songs, and the visits of shepherds and wise men. But is there something more to it than this?

2.1 THE FIRST CHRISTMAS

Christmas is for the children – or is it? Does the birth of Jesus Christ have more to say to us than the tinsel and wrapping paper of the traditional Christmas?

Almost 2,000 years ago, a young woman called Mary lived in Nazareth in Galilee in the land of Palestine. She was engaged to be married to a man called Joseph.

'God saves'

Luke's Gospel tells us that before Mary got married the angel Gabriel appeared to her to tell her that she was going to have a baby. Mary was disturbed by this news. But the angel comforted her. It would happen, not in the usual way, but by God's will and by the power of the Holy Spirit. She would call her son 'Jesus', a Hebrew name meaning 'God saves' or 'Saviour', because this baby would 'save his people from their sins'.

For many years God's people had been looking forward to the coming of 'Messiah', God's 'chosen one', a 'king' who would save Israel. Now the time had come and Mary began to praise God her Saviour.

The birth of Jesus

Palestine was occupied territory — ruled by the Romans. Not long before Mary's baby was due to be born, Augustus, the Roman Emperor, ordered a census to be taken. Everyone had to go to his own city to be counted. Joseph belonged to Bethlehem, known as 'David's city' — Joseph was a descendant of the great king David. So Mary and Joseph travelled to Bethlehem.

Visitors

The noisy, crowded town wasn't the sort of place for a king to be born, but the Gospel accounts tell us that two sets of visitors came to see the baby. Shepherds, who had been told about this marvel by angels, came in from the fields where they had been minding their flocks to see 'the baby lying in a manger'. Wise men, who had studied the stars, travelled from the east to see 'the baby born to be king of the Jews.'

What does the word Christmas mean?

It means 'Christ's mass', from the Old English, Christ's feast day. Although we do not actually know the time of year Jesus was born, from the fourth century, Christians in Rome celebrated the birthday of Jesus on 25 December when the pagan world was having its mid-winter festival. This was held on 25 December or 6 January, according to the calendar used.

Santa Claus makes an unorthodox arrival on the island of Guadeloupe.

Find out

Look at the beginning of Luke's Gospel.
Why did Luke write it?

Look it up

The angel appears to Mary Luke 1:26-28
The shepherds hear the news Luke 2:8-20
The visit of the wise men Matthew 2:1-12

The birth of Jesus

Only two of the four Gospels tell us about the birth of Jesus. Listed here are the events surrounding Jesus' birth.
- **Matthew, Chapters 1-2:**
The ancestors of Jesus
The birth of Jesus
Visitors from the East
The escape to Egypt
The killing of the children
The return from Egypt
- **Luke, Chapters 1-2:**
The birth of John the Baptist announced

The birth of Jesus announced
Mary visits Elizabeth
Mary's song of praise
The birth of John the Baptist
Zechariah's prophecy
The birth of Jesus
The shepherds and angels
Jesus named
Jesus presented in the temple
The return to Nazareth
- **Luke 3:23-38:**
The ancestors of Jesus

The future King

Many years before the birth of Jesus, the prophet Isaiah foretold the coming of a deliverer:
'A Child is born to us!
A Son is given to us!
And he will be our ruler.
He will be called, 'Wonderful Counsellor,' 'Mighty God', 'Eternal Father', 'Prince of Peace'.
Isaiah 9:6

A Christmas Prayer

A Christian's response to the birth of Jesus:
What can I give him,
  Poor as I am?
If I were a shepherd
  I would bring a lamb,
If I were a wise man
  I would do my part, —
Yet what can I give him,
  Give my heart.
Christina Rossetti (1830-1894)

2.2 THE CHILDHOOD OF JESUS

Why don't the Gospels tell us more about the life of Jesus?

Because the Gospels are neither autobiographies nor biographies. They do not tell us the detailed story of Jesus' life. There are no other types of book which are similar to the Gospels. Their aim is to show people the meaning of the life and death of Jesus.

Words

Priest: Simeon was probably a priest in the temple. The privilege of being a priest was passed down from father to son. A priest had the special task of representing the people to God.

Prophet: Anna was a prophet. There are many books by prophets in the Old Testament. A prophet is chosen by God to tell people what God is saying.

Covenant: This refers to the 'agreement' made between God and human beings. One modern example of a covenant is marriage. In the covenant made with Abraham, God promised to care for his 'chosen people'. Jesus came to make a new covenant between God and all people everywhere.

Find out

- How did the three wise men know where to find Jesus? (Matthew 2)
- What is 'oral tradition'?

Look it up

Jesus is named Luke 2:21-38
Herod hears about Jesus Matthew 2:1-16
The boy Jesus in the temple Luke 2:41-52

The four Gospels do not tell us very much about Jesus from the time he was born until he was about thirty years old. But we do know that, like all Jewish boys, Jesus was circumcised and named when he was eight days old. Later he was taken to the temple in Jerusalem to be presented to the Lord — a custom for parents with every firstborn son. There, his parents offered a pair of doves or two young pigeons, as the law required.

God's promise

In the temple they met two old people — Simeon, the priest and Anna, the prophet. These were good, devout people who were waiting for God's promised Messiah. When they saw Jesus they started to praise God, for they recognized him to be Messiah, the 'deliverer', sent to bring God's 'salvation' and 'to set Jerusalem free'.

Escape to Egypt

But Herod the king felt threatened by a baby 'born to be king'. Hearing that he was likely to kill all the baby boys, Mary and Joseph fled with Jesus into Egypt. They returned after Herod's death.

The boy Jesus

Luke's Gospel tells us about Jesus as a boy. Every year, Mary and Joseph went up to Jerusalem for the Passover Festival, along with many other people. When Jesus was twelve years old he went too. He was now old enough to become 'a Son of the Law'. But on the way home his parents found he was missing. Going all the way back to Jerusalem, they found him in the temple sitting with the Jewish

WHO WAS JESUS? 37

Above A Jewish bar mitzvah in Jerusalem. A thirteen-year-old boy comes of age.

Left As a young boy, Jesus would have been taught by a 'Rabbi', or teacher.

teachers, listening to them and asking them questions. Everyone was amazed at his intelligent answers. When his parents expressed concern, he replied, 'Why did you have to look for me? Didn't you know that I had to be in my Father's house?' They didn't understand what he meant.

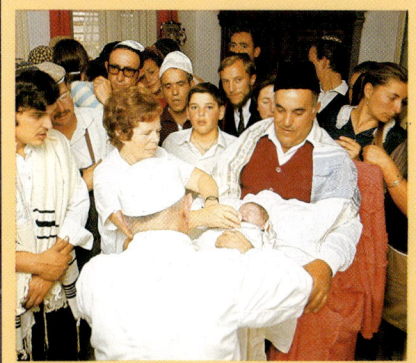

Why were Jewish boys circumcised?
Circumcision involves cutting off the foreskin of the penis. In Genesis we read about how God told Abraham, who started the Jewish nation, that Jewish boys should be circumcised at eight days old as a sign of his covenant with Israel, a sign that they were his 'chosen people', whom he had promised to love and care for.

2.3 WHAT DO WE KNOW ABOUT JESUS?

Archaeologists have unearthed documents, artefacts and even whole cities that tell us how people in the past lived. The ruins of Ephesus, in present-day Turkey, are an important archaeological site.

The key historical evidence for the life of Jesus is found in documents much older than any we have for the ancient classical authors such as Julius Caesar. These documents are the four Gospels: the accounts of the teaching, death and resurrection of Jesus by Matthew, Mark, Luke and John.

The rest of the New Testament (Acts, the Letters, the book of Revelation) has also been shown to be reliable. Scholars have checked out the details of the book of Acts, for instance: they agree with many discoveries made by archaeologists.

WHO WAS JESUS? 39

In these caves at Qumran by the Dead Sea, a collection of scrolls was discovered, dating from around the time of Jesus. The Dead Sea Scrolls have helped to verify the accuracy of the Bible.

People who knew Jesus

And then there is the Christian church — the followers of Jesus. Could the faith of so many millions of people rest on a person who was conjured up by someone's imagination? A man from a legend or myth? A fool or a madman? Could that sort of man inspire a faith so strong that for nearly two thousand years men and women have been willing to die for it?

Jewish and Roman Writers

Outside the New Testament there are a few significant historical references to Jesus:
- **Josephus,** the Jewish historian (about AD 37-100);
- **The Babylonian Talmud,** a collection of Jewish traditions passed on and then written down in the fifth century;
- **Pliny the Younger,** a Latin author (about AD 62-113);
- **Tacitus,** the Roman historian (about AD 55-117);
- **Suetonius,** the Roman writer (about AD 70-160).

Many scholars have puzzled over how the Gospels came to be written: what the sources were, whether one Gospel contradicts another in telling the same story, how we can understand the writer's meaning better.

Amazingly, the documents themselves have withstood the closest study that any documents in history have received! No major Christian belief is threatened by queries about whether bits of the story are authentic or not.

Christians met together on a certain day 'to sing a hymn to Christ as if to a god'.
                  Pliny the Younger

The Emperor Nero tried to put the blame for the great fire which destroyed half the city of Rome in AD 64 on the Christians. Tacitus, who describes Nero's persecution of the Christians in Rome says, 'Their name comes from Christus, who in the reign of Tiberius as emperor was condemned to death by the procurator Pontius Pilate.'
                  Tacitus

Words
Gospel — this really means 'good news'. The four Gospels — Matthew, Mark, Luke and John — were written to tell the good news about Jesus.

Find out ✱
Throughout history there have been Christians willing to die for what they believe. Can you name any of them?

How did the Gospels come to be written?

Matthew, Mark, Luke and John, the four evangelists, used oral and written sources about Jesus to write their Gospels. These are dated somewhere between thirty-five and sixty years after the death of Jesus. Mark's is probably the earliest, and John's is probably the latest, but we don't know for sure.

The oldest fragment of a New Testament book is this one from John's Gospel. Written in Greek, it dates from around AD 125.

For a fuller discussion of the Gospels and the other Bible documents, see Section 5, **God Speaks: The Bible.**

2.4 JESUS BEGINS HIS WORK

Jesus' life

Birth: shortly before the death of Herod the Great in 4 BC.
Baptism: at about the age of 30, probably in AD 27 or 28.
Beginning of public ministry: after his baptism.
Death: at Passover, probably AD 29 or 30.

The message of John the Baptist

'Turn away from your sins and be baptized, and God will forgive your sins.'

'John appeared in the desert, baptizing and preaching... He wore clothes made of camel's hair, with a leather belt round his waist and his food was locusts and wild honey. He announced to the people, "The man who will come after me is much greater than I am. I am not good enough even to bend down and untie his sandals. I baptize you with water, but he will baptize you with the Holy Spirit."'
Mark 1:4,6-8

Jesus did not begin his public ministry — 'the work God gave me to do' he called it — until after his baptism at about thirty years of age. As a young man he probably learnt the carpenter's or 'craftsman's' trade from his father Joseph in Nazareth.

John's baptism

The Jews were expecting a 'saviour', 'deliverer' or 'messiah' (meaning 'anointed one') who would save the country from foreign domination and at the same time crush their enemies. Many believed the Messiah would be a descendant of King David.

At the time Jesus was born, Israel was under Roman rule. So when John, a cousin of Jesus, began preaching in the desert, many came to be 'baptized' — washed in the River Jordan or the pools nearby — thinking he was their Messiah.

John denied the claim. His baptism was of repentance for the forgiveness of sins. His message demanded that people change their ways, turn away from their selfish lives to prepare for one who was still to come, a man much greater than John himself.

The baptism of Jesus

Matthew tells us that when Jesus came to John to be baptized, John was amazed. He exclaimed, 'I ought to be baptized by you and yet you have come to me.'

But Jesus insisted that he too wanted to do what God required and so John agreed. As Jesus

WHO WAS JESUS?

Straight after his baptism, Jesus went out into the desert for forty days.

prayed after his baptism, the heavens opened and the Holy Spirit came down upon him in the form of a dove while a voice announced, 'You are my own dear Son, I am pleased with you.'

The testing of Jesus

Then Jesus was led by the Spirit into the desert where he was tempted by the Devil for forty days. The Devil tempted Jesus to get and use power in a wrong way — to turn stones into bread, to throw himself down from the highest point of the temple without getting hurt, and to accept all the kingdoms of the world and their wealth from the Devil.

Each time, Jesus replied, 'the scripture says . . .' Each time the Devil was defeated. Jesus knew that his power was going to come from serving God alone.

Does God — who is portrayed in the Bible as loving and kind — tempt us to do wrong?
No. God may test us, as a father tests his children or a carpenter tests a chair he has made. He is trying to find out if we can stand up to the test. It is Satan — the Devil — who tries to get us to do wrong.

Think about it . . .
If two trees are blown about in a great storm, the one which does not break bears the most strain.
Think of the times when you have been tempted to do wrong. Which is easier — to give in or to resist? Which of the two helps to build up your character?

Words
Repentance — it really means 'change of mind' or 'change of heart' or to turn away from something. People who repent turn away from their past life to follow Jesus.
Baptism — Jesus commanded his followers to be baptized. In baptism the person is 'washed' or sprinkled with water as a sign of being made clean and starting a new life.

Look it up
Jesus is baptized Matthew 3:13-17
Jesus is tempted Matthew 4:1-11

2.5 GOOD NEWS OF THE KINGDOM

What did Jesus mean by the kingdom?

The Jews expected that Messiah would not only crush their enemies but also rule over them in everlasting peace and prosperity. This was a political hope. But Jesus announced the rule of God over *all* creation and over *all* people. Under God's rule, the whole creation will eventually be restored. In Jesus there began a new age, a fresh start. This was shown as Jesus confronted evil through his preaching, teaching and healing.

After his baptism Jesus spent the next two to three years travelling about the countryside preaching, teaching and healing. Much of that time was spent in Galilee but he travelled to Judea at least twice and perhaps even more frequently.

Forgiveness and new life

The first chapter of Mark's Gospel tells us what Jesus began to do in Galilee. He started announcing the good news.

'The right time has come,' he said, 'and the kingdom of God is near! Turn away from your sins and believe the good news!'

In the coming and preaching of Jesus, God's new rule had begun in the world. People could have their sins forgiven and receive new life. The start of this new life Jesus came to bring is seen in his actions: preaching and teaching, healing, miracles, casting out evil spirits.

Jesus once said, 'I have come to give you life in all its fullness.' To be a Christian means to hear and respond to the good news of Jesus.

Fishermen follow Jesus

As Jesus walked by the shore of Lake Galilee he saw two brothers, Simon and Andrew. They were catching fish with a net. Two other brothers, James and John, were getting their nets ready.

He called all four, saying, 'Come with me and I will teach you to catch men.' They became the first of Jesus' many disciples.

Jesus casts out an evil spirit

Mark tells us that as Jesus taught in the synagogue at Capernaum on the sabbath, a man with an evil spirit cried out. But Jesus ordered the spirit to be quiet and to come out of him. The people were amazed. Who was this man with power and authority to give orders to evil spirits and they obeyed him?

So the news about Jesus spread quickly throughout Galilee.

Jesus heals many people

Simon's mother-in-law was at home in bed sick with a fever when Jesus arrived with his disciples. He took her by the hand and helped her up. Soon she was well enough to wait on them at table.

Later, after the sun had set and evening had come, people came to Jesus. Mark tells us, 'All the people of the town gathered in front of the house.' And Jesus healed many people who were sick and drove out the demons. This was only the start of Jesus' ministry.

Words

Disciple — a follower of Jesus. The word really means a 'learner'. Jesus had many disciples — and the twelve disciples were chosen specially to be close friends.
Sabbath — the day of rest. For Jews this is a Saturday; for Christians it became Sunday because this was the day of the resurrection of Jesus.
Synagogue — the local Jewish meeting-place and (in Jesus' time) school. The main focus was the set of scrolls on which the Jewish law was written.

Jesus' first followers were ordinary working men. There are still fishermen on the Sea of Galilee.

Healing

'One Sunday, a few years ago, I enjoyed spending a Sunday with friends in a church in Kenya. The day began with a baptism by the riverside. Then there was a service of testimony, holy communion and preaching in the church building. At one point the pastor invited anyone who wished to be 'made whole' — to receive healing — to move forward to the altar rails to pray. A mother and her baby came forward. He laid hands on them, and prayed for God's blessing and the healing of body, mind and spirit, as God willed. I felt this showed that God's care for his people is constant and not only when they have a particular illness.'

2.6 GOOD NEWS FOR ALL

Who were the poor?

In Palestine in the time of Jesus a minority led a life of luxury: the rulers and their court, the priestly aristocracy of Jerusalem, wealthy merchants, the chief tax collectors and the great landowners. The middle class was made up of craftsmen and country priests (the small farmers who were often in debt were closer to being peasants). The poorest people were the workers, the day-labourers, the slaves, the unemployed who resorted to begging and the disabled who relied on alms — money collected specially to help poor people.

The poor were those at the bottom of the heap who felt so helpless, powerless and oppressed that they looked to God alone for their deliverance. They believed that when Messiah came, he would proclaim 'God's year of Jubilee (favour)'. This was a time when debts would be cancelled, prisoners set free and land restored to its rightful owners.

The news about Jesus spread throughout the whole of Galilee. He taught in the synagogues and was praised by everyone.

Good news for the poor

One sabbath Jesus went as usual to the synagogue in Nazareth where he had been brought up. It was quite usual to ask any man who was educated to read from the Law and the Prophets in the Old Testament and to deliver a sermon.

Jesus chose a key passage from the prophet Isaiah. At the end of the reading Jesus told them how the prophecy had come true — that very day!

The people were impressed and astonished. God's kingdom, the time of the Messiah, had come, bringing healing, forgiveness and liberation . . .

Jesus is rejected

As they listened further they began to have doubts. Surely this man Jesus was only the son of Joseph? So Jesus reminded them that no prophet was ever welcome in his home town. Even the prophet Elijah was sent by God in a time of famine to a place outside Israel. The prophet Elisha was sent to heal Naaman the Syrian's skin-disease even though there were many who needed healing in Israel.

Jesus in the synagogue at Nazareth

Jesus stood up to read from the prophet Isaiah.
'The Spirit of the Lord has been given
   to me,
for he has anointed me,
He has sent me to bring the good
   news to the poor,
to proclaim liberty to captives
and to the blind new sight,
to set the downtrodden free,
to proclaim the Lord's year of favour.'
Luke 4:18-19, quoting from Isaiah 61:1-2 and 58:6

What Jesus meant was clear: this message of healing, forgiveness and liberation could be rejected by Israel — God's 'chosen people' — and offered to the Gentiles. In fact, Jesus had not finished the quotation from Isaiah. He had not mentioned the day of vengeance which Jews felt would fall on Gentiles, while they themselves would be saved.

So the people in the synagogue became very angry and dragged Jesus out of town to the top of a cliff to throw him down. But Jesus slipped through the crowd and walked away.

Who were the Gentiles?
The Gentiles were the nations other than God's 'chosen people' Israel. They were the non-Jews. Because they were God's 'chosen people', the Jews were supposed to show the Gentiles what God is like. This is a responsibility they often failed to take on. See the story of Jonah for instance — Jonah ran away from the idea of preaching to the great Gentile city of Nineveh.

A group of Christians meet to study the Bible.

Good news for the world

One of the themes in the Gospels is that Jesus came *first* to the people of Israel. But this does not mean that the good news is only for the Jewish people — it is for the whole world. Luke's Gospel makes a special point of this.

Think about it...
Why do you think the people in Nazareth, Jesus' home town, rejected him?

Check ✓
What was the sabbath?
What was a synagogue?

Look it up
The events recorded in this chapter are from Luke, chapter 4.

2.7 JESUS THE TEACHER

Teaching in an African school. Jesus, too, was a teacher. But his classroom was wherever he could get a hearing, and his students were those who sometimes travelled miles to hear him.

Jesus says goodbye

In John's Gospel (chapters 14-17) Jesus tells his disciples that he will soon be leaving them. Yet they must not be upset because he is going ahead to prepare a place for them in heaven. In the meantime he will send them 'a Comforter', the Holy Spirit. The Spirit will come alongside them to strengthen and encourage them. He will make them continually aware of the presence of Jesus. He will also teach them and lead them to the truth. Then, at the end, Jesus himself will return and take them home to be with him for ever.

After the death of Jesus and at Pentecost (the coming of the Holy Spirit) Jesus' disciples remembered those words.

Jesus was a brilliant teacher. He was always watching what was going on round about him. So when he came to teach, he used real-life situations to bring his stories to life. People flocked round him. He always had something interesting and exciting to say.

The Sermon on the Mount

In his Sermon on the Mount Jesus delivered a new 'law'. It is a law of love. It does not contradict the Law of the Old Testament but develops the spirit underlying the Ten Commandments. Jesus' followers should:
● set their hearts first of all on God's kingdom and God's righteousness;
● love their enemies as well as their neighbours;
● be 'the salt of the earth' — no longer tasteless;
● be 'the light of the world' — no longer hidden.

It is what lies behind the Law that matters, Jesus said. For example: 'You have heard that people were told in the past, "Do not commit murder; anyone who does will be brought to trial." But now I tell you: whoever is angry with his brother will be brought to trial . . .'

The two builders

Jesus then told a story about two builders. The person who listens to Jesus' words and acts on them is like a wise man who builds his house on rock, but the person who listens and does not act on them is like a man who builds his house on sand. When the storms come on, one stands, the other falls.

For the small group of disciples, the teaching of Jesus was revolutionary. It turned accepted standards upside down. It is not the rich and famous who are happy; it is those who are pure in heart, the helpless, those who hunger and thirst for what is right . . .

True Happiness

Happy are the poor in spirit;
   theirs is the kingdom of heaven.
Happy are those who mourn;
   they shall be comforted.
Happy are those who are helpless;
   they shall have the earth for their heritage.
Happy are those who hunger and thirst for what is right;
   they shall be satisfied.
Happy are the merciful;
   they shall have mercy shown them.
Happy are the pure in heart;
   they shall see God.
Happy are the peacemakers;
   they shall be called children of God.
Happy are those who are persecuted in the cause of right;
   theirs is the kingdom of heaven.
Happy are you when people insult you and persecute you
   and speak all kinds of evil against you on my account.
Jesus, in Matthew 5:3-11

The Lord's Prayer

Jesus taught his disciples how to pray:
'Our Father in heaven:
May your holy name be honoured;
may your kingdom come;
may your will be done on earth as it is in heaven.
Give us today the food we need.
Forgive us the wrongs we have done, as we forgive the wrongs that others have done to us.
Do not bring us to hard testing but keep us safe from the Evil One.'
Jesus, in Matthew 6:9-13

Stories with a point

Jesus' most outstanding teaching is contained in his parables. These are lively stories, based on real-life situations. Jesus used them to put across a single point — something which invited a response.

God's kingdom is like . . .

Jesus used parables to tell a series of picture-stories about God's kingdom. Each story begins: 'God's kingdom is like . . .'
- A man takes the smallest of seeds, a mustard seed, and plants it in the ground. After a while it grows and becomes the biggest of all plants, putting out such large branches that the birds come and make nests in its shade.
- A woman takes yeast and mixes it with flour. Yeast spreads and makes the bread rise.
- Treasure is hidden in a field. Someone finds it and covers it up again quickly. He goes away happy, and sells everything he owns to buy the field.
- A merchant is looking for fine pearls. When he finds one of great value, he sells everything he owns and buys it.

- A dragnet is cast into the sea. When it is full, the fishermen haul it ashore. Then they collect the good fish in a basket and throw away those which are of no use. This is how it will be at the end of time when the evil people will be separated from the good people.

So, God's rule:
- grows from small beginnings;
- brings joy and is very valuable;
- will separate good from evil at the end of time.

Lost and found

God does not say, 'If you are good, then I will love you.' His love reaches out to sinners and outcasts. Jesus showed this in three parables — the lost sheep, the lost coin and the lost son (see Luke chapter 15). The message of the stories is that God seeks, finds and welcomes home those who are 'lost'. God's love is not earned — it is freely offered to all who want to receive it. This is important (and difficult) for people today who think that you have to be good to be a Christian or be accepted by God.

If God is our Father and he wants to show his love for us by giving us gifts, why do we need to pray?
Because, like our parents, God likes us to show our love and dependence on him by saying 'please' and 'thanks'.

Left Jesus used ordinary, everyday events to teach people about God. In many respects, everyday life in the Middle East has changed little since Jesus' time. Here a Bedouin woman from Jordan makes unleavened bread.

Think about it . . .
Look at each verse of True Happiness (sometimes called the Beatitudes). Are these things still important in our world today? Why?

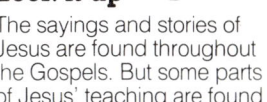

Look it up

The sayings and stories of Jesus are found throughout the Gospels. But some parts of Jesus' teaching are found in blocks of chapters:
The Sermon on the Mount Matthew 5-7
The parables of the kingdom Matthew 13
Jesus predicts the end Luke 21
Jesus says goodbye to his disciples and prepares them for the future John 14-17

The lost sheep
The lost coin
The lost son
In Luke 15

2.8 JESUS THE HEALER

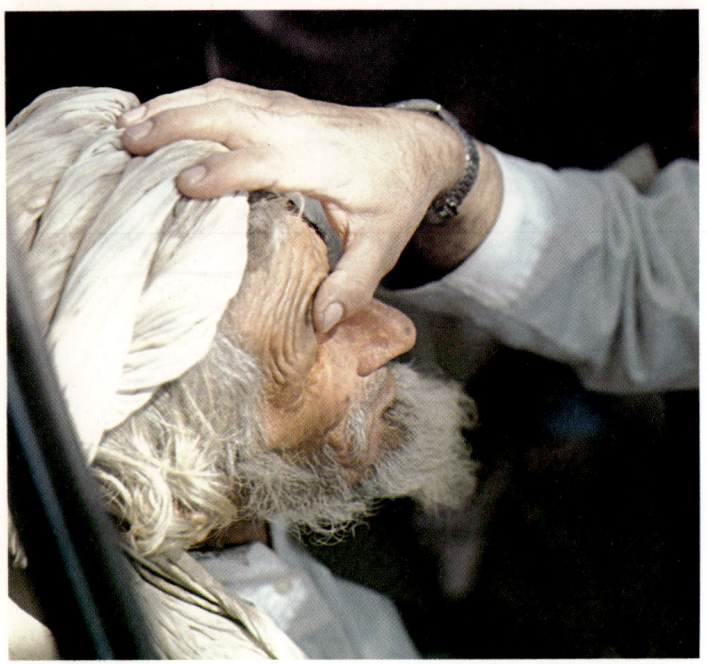

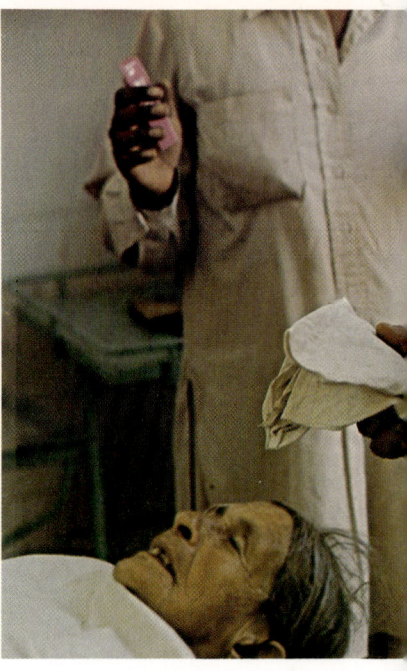

Jesus responded to human need by healing those who were ill. Modern Christians follow him in their medical work. Here a patient is examined at a roadside clinic in Pakistan.

When he healed people, Jesus showed his great love and compassion towards all who suffered. But he not only healed bodily diseases — he also forgave sins. The forgiveness of sins showed that Jesus came to bring healing for the whole person — healing of the body and of the mind and spirit.

In other words, when Jesus healed people and forgave their sins, it was a sign of complete healing, of wholeness. All need to be forgiven — some need to be made well too.

There are many accounts of Jesus healing people in the Gospels.

Jesus heals a paralyzed man

One day Jesus was in Capernaum. Immediately the word got round. So many people arrived at the house to see Jesus that there was no room, even around the front door.

While Jesus was teaching inside, four men carrying a friend on a mat arrived. Because they could not get in by the door, they took the paralyzed man up on to the roof, made a hole in it and let him down into the house!

When Jesus saw their faith he said to the man, 'My son, your sins are forgiven.' When some of the scribes objected to Jesus' forgiving sins, Jesus just told the man to pick up his mat and walk. This was as much as to ask 'What's the difference?'

Jesus heals a blind man

As Jesus was walking along with his disciples he saw a man who had been blind from birth. 'Teacher,' asked his disciples, 'whose sin caused him to be born blind, his own or his parents?'

'Neither,' replied Jesus, 'he was born blind so that God's power might be seen at work in him.' And with these words he spat on the ground, made a paste, spread it

> **Think about it . . .**
> Did Jesus classify people as 'good' and 'bad'?
> What was his response to them? Why?

Look it up
Jesus heals a paralyzed man Mark 2:1-12
Jesus heals a blind man John 9:1-12

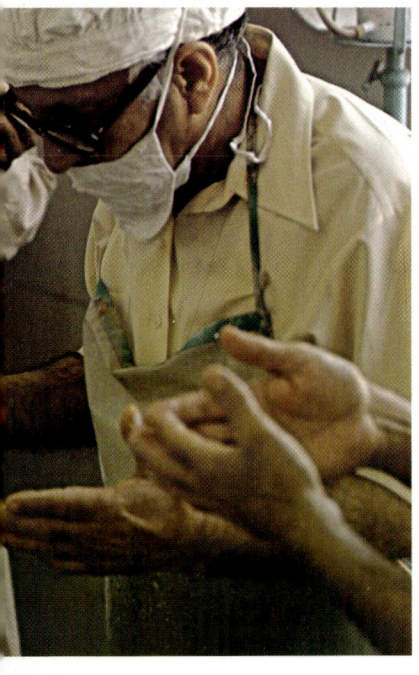

over the eyes of the blind man and said to him, 'Go and wash in the Pool of Siloam.' So the blind man went away, washed himself and came back seeing.

This caused an uproar among the people — and an investigation by the Pharisees, who held the view that illness must be caused by sin. They thought that 'bad' people deserved their suffering, while 'good' people (like themselves) deserved God's favour.

Jesus responded to this by saying, 'It is not those who are well who need a doctor, but those who are sick.'

Left A Christian doctor in Pakistan prays with his patient before performing a cataract operation.

Why did people flock to see Jesus?

In all the Gospel accounts Jesus showed great love and pity towards anybody in need. His love was acted out in making people 'whole' — healthy and renewed in body, mind and spirit. This wholeness was a sign that in Jesus God's kingdom had come.

Sin and suffering

In Bible times it was widely believed that there was a direct connection between sin and suffering, righteousness and success, long life, large families and being rich. Long life and riches were associated with God's favour; misfortune, disease and poverty were thought to be due to God's displeasure.

In the Old Testament the book of Job took up this theme — and said it wasn't true! Job's misfortunes and illness were not due to his behaviour — he was a good and righteous man. Job never knew the reason for his suffering — but he did learn something about the sovereign power and wisdom of God. Certainly sin in general has led to illness and suffering. But a person's illness or misfortune are not necessarily because of individual sin.

Human suffering is a fact that cannot be ignored. This German war cemetery from World War II contains 12,000 graves.

2.9 JESUS THE MIRACLE WORKER

The Gospels tell us about many miracles which Jesus did. He appears to have had extraordinary power over nature, evil spirits and all kinds of diseases.

The words or phrases used to describe these supernatural acts, or miracles, are 'mighty works', 'wonders' and 'signs'.

● **Mighty works** emphasize the great power which Jesus had, which he said came from God his Father.

● **Wonders** show the wonder and amazement of the people who witnessed his miracles.

● **Signs** refer to the coming of God's kingdom which Jesus showed in his miracles. Satan, the enemy of God, is being challenged and put to flight. Such miraculous signs, as the Jewish people well knew, were only to be expected with the coming of God's kingdom. So what Jesus *did* backed up what he *said* about himself.

Calming the storm

Jesus showed his power over the forces of nature. He was crossing the Lake of Galilee in a boat with his disciples. Suddenly a strong wind blew up and the waves began to spill over into the boat, so that it was about to fill with water. A sudden storm like this was quite common.

The disciples were frightened,

Healing today

This is an account of healing in Indonesia today.

'Dr Sung encouraged the sick to realize that healing depended on the will of the Lord. He said, 'I cannot guarantee that all the sick among you will be healed. Even the Lord Jesus did not heal all the sick . . .'

After these introductory remarks the sick were then brought up to Dr Sung on the large platform one by one. As they knelt he anointed them each with oil in the name of the Lord and prayed with them.

That same afternoon a praise meeting was held in which those who had been healed gave their testimonies. Many had been cured of serious illnesses. A missionary wrote later, 'Blind people received their sight, the lame walked, the dumb spoke, the ears of the deaf were opened; and best of all, the cures have lasted.' So it was not just a case of auto-suggestion.
Kurt Koch

then annoyed as they saw Jesus sleeping with his head on a pillow at the back of the boat. 'Teacher, don't you care that we are about to die?' they cried out. Yet, when Jesus stood up and calmed the wind and the waves, and rebuked his disciples for their lack of faith, they were afraid, wondering what kind of man he was 'that even the wind and the waves obey him.'

Exorcising the spirits

On several occasions Jesus cast out evil spirits from people. So his power was over not only the forces of nature, but the forces of evil too. This was evidence of the final victory over evil that Jesus would win on the cross, and evidence of God's rule.

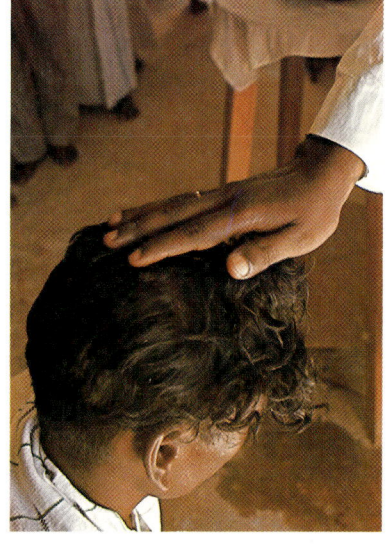

Jesus often healed people by touching them. On several occasions he touched lepers – an action that was both socially unacceptable and dangerous.

Jesus even brought someone back to life. Lazarus had been buried for three days. Jesus was looking forward to the triumph of the resurrection, when he was raised from the dead. Jesus showed that he has power over life and death.

But even at the time of Jesus, like today, not everyone was healed. Jesus did not stop the whole process of illness and death — then. But it was to be only a matter of time! In the new age of his kingdom, suffering and death would be gone for ever.

So in the miracles of Jesus, and in Christian healing today, we catch a glimpse of the age to come.

How was Jesus different from other exorcists in his time?

Jesus cast out evil spirits by the word and power of God (the 'Spirit of God', the 'finger of God') as a sign of God's authority and rule over the powers of evil.

Despite our hopes and dreams, and our plans for the future, the only thing we can be completely certain about is that we will one day die. The Christian faith can help us to make sense of death, and to give us a hope that looks beyond it.

Look it up

Roman officer's servant
Luke 7:1-10
The man from Gadara
Mark 5:1-15
Calming the storm
Matthew 8:23-27
Walking on the water Mark 6:48-51

2.10 JESUS BRINGS CONFLICT!

Jesus was popular with the common people — for most of the time. But he was often out of favour with the power groups and special interest groups — the 'political' groups.

In Palestine there were many different groups — social, religious and political — which were not always on good terms either with one another or with the Romans, the occupying power. Jesus seems to have come into conflict with most of them — partly because they picked quarrels with him, but also because what Jesus did and said was controversial and revolutionary.

Picking a fight

From the beginning, the doctors of the Law, most of whom were Pharisees, found fault with Jesus.

Walking through some cornfields on the sabbath day with his disciples, Jesus did not stop them plucking ears of corn, rubbing them in their palms and eating them. The Pharisees objected to this — it was like threshing the grain and therefore not allowed on the sabbath!

Jesus replied that the sabbath was made for man's benefit and not man for the sabbath.

In the same way Jesus ignored objections to the healings he did on the sabbath. Surely it was better to do good rather than evil — even on the sabbath? This was only one of the many incidents recorded in the Gospels.

The Sadducees were even more hostile to Jesus than the scribes and Pharisees. They tried to trap Jesus in arguments about religious questions.

The followers of Herod Antipas — collaborators with the Roman rule — also tried to trap Jesus by asking him awkward questions.

The Pharisees, Sadducees and Herodians thought of themselves as important people — people with authority, especially about the Law.

A man of authority

Jesus had an air of authority — no one who ever met him could deny it. All the arguments about the Law seem to start from this point. Where did Jesus' authority come from?

Think about it . . .
Read Mark 7:14-23. Do you agree with what Jesus says? Is it still true today?

Look it up

Jesus always had a ready answer to those who tried to trap him with trick questions — it wasn't always the answer they expected!
- **John 8:1-11** The Pharisees bring a woman who has committed adultery.
- **Matthew 22:15-22** The Pharisees ask Jesus about paying taxes.
- **Mark 12:18-27** The Sadducees ask Jesus about resurrection.

The religious groups

- **The Pharisees**

The Pharisees were the 'separated ones', who kept themselves apart from what was displeasing to God. They were usually good men, concerned for the holiness of God and the keeping of the Law. Through difficult times they had kept the true faith of Israel alive.

But their failing was 'legalism' — thinking that they could rely on keeping the Law to earn them a place in heaven. They had great zeal for keeping the Law in every little detail. But often it was just 'play-acting' — the original meaning of the word Jesus used of them — hypocrites.

- **The Sadducees**

The Sadducees were priestly aristocrats. They willingly collaborated with the Roman occupying forces for their own benefit. They were wealthy and worldly.

We are not certain of their beliefs. They appear to have accepted only the first five books of the Old Testament (known as the Pentateuch or the Torah) as authoritative, rejecting the oral law of the scribes and doctors of the Law. They did not believe in the resurrection of the dead. They behaved extremely harshly towards the common people and were among the greatest opponents of Jesus.

WANTED
THESE MEN ARE DANGEROUS

OSCAR ROMERO

Oscar Romero was a dangerous man. But he is no longer dangerous — because he is dead. He was a shy, quiet man, and the politicians of El Salvador who made him Archbishop thought they could easily manipulate him. They were wrong.

As Archbishop, Romero began to speak out in sermons and on the radio against violence, whether by government forces or left-wing groups. In March 1980 he was gunned down by four masked men as he celebrated mass. According to one report, his last words were: 'May Christ's sacrifice give us the courage to offer our own bodies for justice and peace.'

DIETRICH BONHOEFFER

When Adolf Hitler came to power in Germany in 1933, Dietrich Bonhoeffer, along with many other Christians, opposed him. He became active in the anti-Hitler resistance movement and spoke out against the inhuman Nazi policies.

In 1939 he refused a job offered to him in the United States — which would have given him a safe life. Instead he stayed in Germany, became a double-agent and was involved in a plot to assassinate Hitler. He was arrested in 1943 by the Gestapo for smuggling fourteen Jews out of the country to Switzerland.

He was hanged two years later, only weeks before the end of the war.

VALERI BARINOV

When Valeri Barinov wrote his rock opera, *Trumpet Call*, he did not realize what trouble it would cause him. For Barinov is a Christian and a Soviet citizen. At first, he was refused permission to perform the opera. When he appealed, his problems really started.

He was put under twenty-four-hour surveillance. Then he was arrested and committed to a psychiatric unit. His wife was told that his illness was 'abnormal beliefs'. He was injected daily with Larcactil — a powerful drug known to cause drowsiness and liver damage. There is no doubt that his arrest was directly connected with his Christian beliefs.

Valeri has now been sentenced to two and a half years in a labour camp.

DESMOND TUTU

Desmond Tutu is a Nobel Peace Prize winner and the Bishop of Johannesburg. But he is black. He is dangerous because he openly voices his opposition to the apartheid system of South Africa.

Why is the black majority in South Africa ruled by a minority of whites? Why are black people treated as an inferior race? Why are many men forced to live apart from their wives and children eleven months a year? And why are protesters imprisoned without trial?

Asking questions like these makes Desmond Tutu dangerous. People who say things like this have been arrested.

2.11 FRIEND OF SINNERS

Jesus got into most trouble because he made friends with social outcasts — people whom nobody wanted. Respectable people were horrified to see Jesus and his disciples mixing with tax collectors and sinners, women and foreigners — considered to be the lowest people in society!

Tax collectors and sinners

Tax collectors were despised — they collected taxes for the Romans. They were also well known for taking more than their due — and pocketing the money.

One of the disciples was a tax collector before he left his job to follow Jesus. Zacchaeus, the little man who climbed up the sycamore tree to see Jesus, was a terrible cheat. But when Jesus invited himself to his home for a meal, Zacchaeus changed — he promised to repay people fourfold.

Samaritans and foreigners

There are stories in the Gospels which tell us that Jesus was ready to heal 'foreigners' as well as Jews.

Jews despised Samaritans: so when Jesus made a Samaritan the hero in one of his best known parables — 'The *Good* Samaritan' — people were scandalized.

Women

Jesus' attitude to women was revolutionary for a Jew and a teacher, a 'rabbi', of his time. Women were not regarded highly — they were definitely second-class citizens.

Jesus got on well with women. His relationship to them was easy and natural. He allowed women to touch him, accompany him, serve him and listen to his teaching.

Think about it . . .
- Is Jesus' attitude to women relevant to today's world?
- List reasons why you think Jesus said that a rich man would find it impossible to 'inherit the kingdom of God'. Might the same be true today?

Look it up
The woman at the well John 4:5-30
The woman with the haemorrhage Mark 5:25-34
The Gentile woman's daughter is healed Matthew 15:21-28
Jesus with Martha and Mary Luke 10:38-42
Jesus at the house of Simon the Pharisee Luke 7:36-50
The resurrection Luke 24:1-12

Jesus and women

In his time, Jesus' attitude to women was completely revolutionary:

- At a well in Samaria Jesus allowed a woman with a bad reputation (three times an outsider by virtue of being a Samaritan, a woman and a 'sinner'!) to give him a drink and talk to him in public. No wonder that both the woman

and the disciples were amazed and shocked.

- In a dense crowd he healed a woman with a haemorrhage who had touched him. By Jewish tradition she should not have touched him; and men would be considered ritually impure from her touch.

- In the border region of Tyre and Sidon — a 'foreign country' — he encouraged a Gentile woman to ask for her daughter's healing. He answered her plea with compassion and gentle humour.

- In the house of Mary and Martha at Bethany he praised Mary for sitting at his feet like a student at the feet of a teacher or rabbi. Jesus told her sister Martha off for being over-anxious about housework. Far from saying that a woman's place is in the home, Jesus' criticism was for a woman who was over-busy in the home.

- In Simon the Pharisee's house he allowed a sinful woman to wet his feet with her tears, wipe them with her hair and anoint them with precious ointment.

- At the resurrection he appeared first to the women and told them to announce the good news to his disciples.

2.12 FOLLOW ME!

Jesus' first words to his disciples were 'follow me!' The early Christians were known as 'followers of the Way'. Christians are people who walk in Jesus' footsteps.

The twelve disciples

'Jesus called his disciples to him and chose twelve of them to be apostles:
Simon (whom he named Peter)
and his brother Andrew;
James and John,
Philip and Bartholomew,
Matthew and Thomas,
James son of Alphaeus,
and Simon (who was called the Zealot),
Judas son of James,
and Judas Iscariot, who became the traitor.'
Luke 6:13-16

Jesus had many followers. There are three groups who are particularly mentioned in the Gospels:
- the women who were his friends, such as Mary and Martha of Bethany;
- the seventy disciples sent out on a special mission;
- the twelve 'disciples' or 'apostles' whom he chose to be very close to him. To these twelve he gave a special responsibility — telling people about him.

The disciples

The twelve disciples were a mixed bunch from varied backgrounds, different occupations, with different characteristics and personalities. The New Testament gives us vivid pictures of some of them, but we do not know very much about others. James, John, Simon and Andrew, were fishermen. They probably owned their own boats and had a flourishing business. Yet they left all that to follow Jesus.

- **James and John**, nicknamed by Jesus 'sons of thunder', are known for their stormy temperament and desire for power and greatness.
- **Andrew** is remembered for his interest in bringing others to Jesus.
- **Simon** (whom Jesus surnamed Peter, 'the rock') is the character who comes over most strongly in the New Testament. He is a man of action, the leader. He is impetuous, full of good intentions. He recognizes that Jesus is the Messiah. He swears everlasting loyalty — yet at the time of Jesus' trial, he denies even knowing him. Nevertheless, after the resurrection Jesus gives Peter the task of looking after his 'sheep' — the followers of Jesus.
- **Matthew**, also known as Levi, was a tax collector when Jesus called him. He became, as far as we know, a loyal follower, and is named as author of the first Gospel.
- **Simon the Zealot** belonged to a nationalist group whose aim was to overthrow the Romans and free Israel.
- **Judas Iscariot** was the 'keeper of the purse', the group's treasurer — and the one who betrayed Jesus. Certainly in the Gospels he is portrayed as the kind of person who was ready to sell his Master for 'thirty pieces of silver'.
- **Philip** came from the same lakeside town of Bethsaida in Galilee as Simon Peter and Andrew. It was Philip who told Bartholomew that he had found the Messiah and who, with Andrew, brought the boy with five loaves and two fishes to Jesus.
- **Thomas** has been nicknamed 'doubting Thomas'. After Jesus' resurrection he was not present on one of the occasions when Jesus appeared to his followers. Thomas said he was unconvinced about the resurrection unless he could touch Jesus physically. When, eventually, he did see Jesus he simply exclaimed 'My Lord, and my God'.
- Of the remaining three disciples, **Bartholomew**, **James** the son of Alphaeus and **Judas** the son of James, we know nothing for certain.

Think about it . . .
What does Jesus' choice of special friends tell us about him?

Find out
Look up the following stories about Simon Peter.
What kind of man was he?
Matthew 4:18-19
Mark 8:27-30
Matthew 26:31-35
Matthew 26:69-75
John 21:1-19

PICTURING JESUS

Above Jesus has been pictured in many different ways down the ages. This medieval stained-glass view of Christ is in Canterbury Cathedral, England and dates from the thirteenth century.

Above Scenes from the life of Jesus are carved on this church door in Nigeria.

Above A nineteenth century depiction of Jesus that claims to be completely accurate.

Right Jesus as seen by a Chinese painter. This painting, on silk, shows Jesus teaching Mary Magdalene.

Above An African Jesus in Ethiopian stained-glass. Each culture sees Jesus as 'one of us', and not as a foreigner.

Below 'The Light of the World' by the nineteenth century English artist Holman Hunt.

Left A Roman Catholic statue of Jesus from Peru.

Below A Greek Orthodox icon showing the virgin Mary with the infant Jesus. It is not just a pretty picture. It is more like 'a window into and out of heaven'. Someone has said, 'You don't look at an icon. It looks at you.'

Left An eleventh century face of Christ from Alsace, France.

2.13 THE COST OF FOLLOWING JESUS

Christians meet to worship in Bucharest, Romania. This country is an atheistic state that actively opposes all Christian activity. The cost of following Jesus is extremely high for many people in today's world.

Think about it . . .
Make a list of reasons why someone might find it difficult to follow Jesus today.

Many people in Jesus' time, including the twelve disciples, went on believing that the Messiah's kingdom would be an earthly one, following an earthly pattern with rulers and ruled, high and low.

Called to serve

From the very beginning of his ministry — the time of testing in the desert — Jesus rejected the kind of power used by the political and religious leaders of his day.

His kingdom, his rule, would be different. Power and authority would be turned upside down. Instead of the leaders telling everyone else what to do, leadership would be by serving. The one who wants to be great must be the servant of the rest, and the one who wants to be first must be the last of all.

Called to carry the cross

Crucifixion, being nailed to a cross to die, was a cruel Roman method of execution. Criminals on their way to the place of crucifixion had to carry the cross-beam of their cross on their back.

Jesus used this picture when he warned his disciples of the cost of following him. Anyone wishing to follow Jesus must take up his cross daily — be prepared even to die for him.

'Whoever wants to save his own life will lose it; but whoever loses his life for me and for the gospel will save it,' Jesus said.

Called to sacrifice

The story of the rich young ruler shows us what Jesus asks of his followers.

This young man was happy to keep the commandments, yet he was concerned about eternal life. When Jesus challenged him and suggested that he sell all his possessions and give them to the poor, his face fell. And we read that he went away sad, because he was very rich.

So following Jesus has a cost. But, because God's values are not the same as the world's, no follower of Jesus ever finds the cost is too much.

One prayer puts it this way, 'To serve you is perfect freedom.'

Top *A baptismal service held in secret in the countryside in the Soviet Union. These Christians can face severe penalties for practising their faith in this way.*

Bottom *A group of Christians meet to pray and read the Bible together in China. Despite official persecution for many years, the Chinese church is strong and growing. Restrictions have started to be lifted.*

The Great Commandments

Jesus was probably the first to bring the commands to love God and neighbour together in the great commandments of love: '"Love the Lord your God with all your heart, with all your soul, and with all your mind." This is the greatest and most important commandment. The second most important commandment is like it: "Love your neighbour as you love yourself."'
Matthew 22:37-39

The New Commandment

'Jesus said to his disciples: "A new commandment I give to you, that you love one another as I have loved you. If you love one another, then everyone will know that you are my disciples."'
John 13:34-35

Sending Out the Seventy

Jesus also chose seventy disciples and sent them out two by two, to go ahead of him to every town and place where he himself was about to go. He said to them, 'There is a large harvest, but few workers to gather it in. Pray to the owner of the harvest that he will send out workers to gather in his harvest. Go! I am sending you like lambs among wolves. Don't take a purse or a beggar's bag or shoes; don't stop to greet anyone on the road. Whenever you go into a house, first say, "Peace be with this house."'
Luke 10:1-5

Look it up
Following Jesus Mark 8:34-36
The rich man Luke 18:18-30

2.14 JESUS FACES DEATH

Jesus predicts his death

'Jesus began to teach his disciples: "The Son of Man must suffer much and be rejected by the elders, the chief priests, and the teachers of the law. He will be put to death, but three days later he will rise to life." He made this very clear to them.'
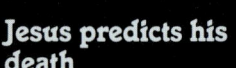
Mark 8:31-32

By now we can see that Jesus was not like the Messiah which most of the Jews expected. He did not want to be a political ruler, a king of the Jews to throw out the Romans and rule over an earthly kingdom. But this was not at all clear to the twelve disciples.

Peter's declaration

One day Jesus asked them who the people said he was.

They promptly replied, 'Some say that you are John the Baptist, others say that you are Elijah, while others say that you are one of the prophets.'

So then Jesus asked them, 'What about you? Who do you say I am?'

And Peter immediately answered, 'You are the Messiah.'

But when Jesus began to prepare his disciples for his death it was Peter who took Jesus aside to rebuke him. Jesus knew that the elders, chief priests and doctors of the law would reject him, make him suffer and put him to death. Then, after three days, he would rise again. But Peter could not believe that this would happen.

Keep it a secret

In Mark's Gospel Jesus is portrayed as wanting his Messiahship kept secret. So Jesus tells his disciples not to let anyone know who he is, just as he had told the evil spirits, when they recognized him, not to tell others. Mark also tells us that the disciples did not really understand what Jesus was talking about.

The transfiguration

The transfiguration is the turning point in the Gospels' presentation of Jesus: Mark tells us that Jesus told Peter, James and John not to talk about it until after 'the Son of Man has risen from death'.

Jesus had taken the 'inner circle' of three up to a high mountain. Before them, he was changed into a shining figure, seen in conversation with Moses and Elijah, representing the Law and the Prophets of the Old Testament. Then a cloud appeared and covered them with its shadow, and a voice said from the cloud, 'This is my own dear Son — listen to him!'

The incident is usually seen as a foretaste of Jesus' glory after the resurrection.

But first he had to go to death — a horrible death, nailed to a cross.

Find out

Read Mark 1:21-28,40-45; 5:1-20; 8:22-30; 9:30-32.

Why does it seem that Jesus did not want to let people think he was the Messiah?

The Jews rejected many of the prophets sent by God. Who were they? What happened to them?

Look it up

Peter's declaration Matthew 16:13-20
The Transfiguration Mark 9:2-9

2.15 ON TO JERUSALEM

The death of Jesus was no accident. Jesus deliberately went up to Jerusalem, knowing that his enemies were plotting his arrest and death.

When Jesus spoke to the twelve disciples about the cost of following him and about the nearness of his death, they were all travelling together towards Jerusalem. John's Gospel actually tells us that Jesus set out for Jerusalem in order to die.

A prophecy comes true

In the Old Testament, Zechariah the prophet, in looking forward to the coming Messiah, had written:

'**Tell the city of Zion,
   Look, your king is coming to you!
He is humble and rides on a donkey
   and on a colt, the foal of a donkey.'**
Zechariah 9:9, quoted in Matthew 21:5

In this way Matthew explains why Jesus sent two of his disciples to a village near Jerusalem to get 'a donkey tied up with her colt beside her'. The prophecy is about to be fulfilled: Jesus is to enter Jerusalem as a humble king riding on a donkey! Can this be the Messiah the Jewish people have been waiting for?

Jesus loved Jerusalem

When Jesus was warned to leave Galilee because Herod wanted to kill him, he said, 'I must be on my way today, tomorrow, and the next day; it is not right for a prophet to be killed anywhere except in Jerusalem' and continued:

'**Jerusalem, Jerusalem! You kill the prophets, you stone the messengers God has sent you! How many times have I wanted to put my arms round all your people, just as a hen gathers her chicks under her wings, but you would not let me! And so your Temple will be abandoned. I assure you that you will not see me until the time comes when you say, "God bless him who comes in the name of the Lord."'**
Jesus, in Luke 13:34-35